better together*

*This book is best read together, grownup and kid.

 akidsbookabout.com

a kids book about™ MONEY

by Adam Stramwasser

a kids book about™

Library of Congress Cataloging-in-Publication Data is available.

This book represents my personal experience and knowledge and thus is not intended to be representative everything there is to know about money.

A Kids Book About Money is exclusively available online on the a kids book about website.

To share your stories, ask questions, or inquire about bulk purchases (schools, libraries, and non-profits), please use the following email address:

hello@akidsbookabout.com

www.akidsbookabout.com

ISBN: 978-1-951253-01-1

Printed in the USA

Interested in inviting Adam Stramwasser to speak at your school?

Visit TopYouthSpeakers.com

To Michelle

Intro

There's nothing like seeing kids smile and enjoy life. But sometimes, the things we do to try to make them happy might come with some unintended consequences.

The gifts we give them, the way we respond to their wants, how we let them treat their toys, and how we talk (or don't talk) about money are all teaching them something, good or bad, about the value of things.

Money can be complicated, even for us as grownups. So understandably, many of us avoid talking to kids about it. But the reality, whether we like it or not, is that kids are forming their own ideas around money just by watching us.

This book is designed to help you, the grownup in their life, shape those ideas and help them understand the importance of consciously saving, spending, and giving.

Hi, my name is Adam.

And this is a kids book
about money.

Let's try something...

say:

DEE-NEH-ROH

Congratulations, now you speak Spanish!

"Dinero" is Spanish for...

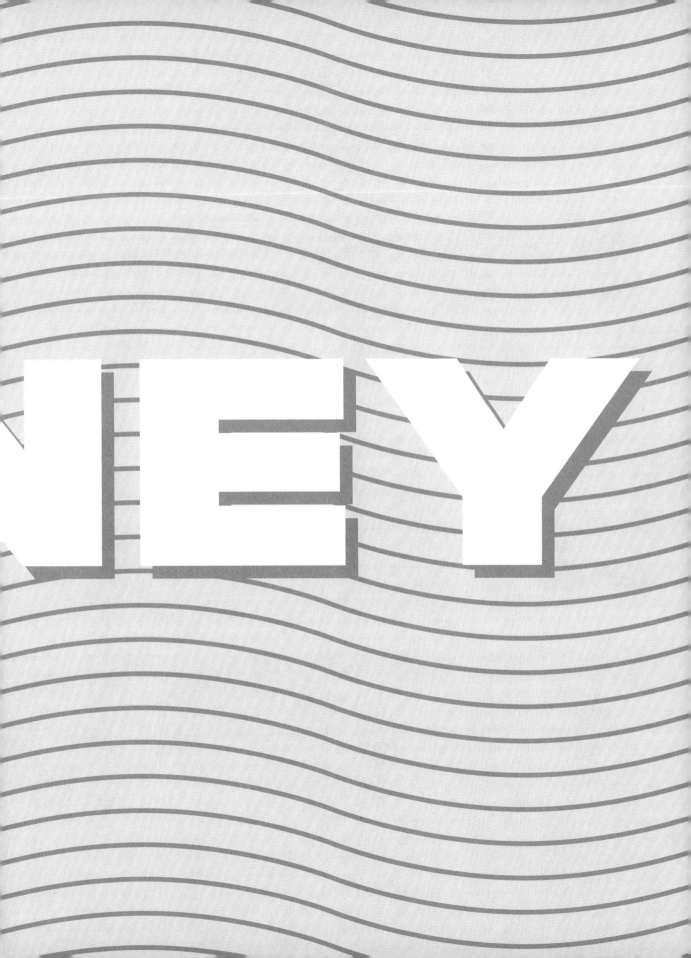

Money can be...

We carry money...

Bills
Coins
Digital Coins
Checks

In a wallet
On bank cards
On a phone
On our watch

Have you ever wondered...

Where money comes from?

Why we need money?

What money can buy?

How to get more money?

Money can be really

even for grownups...

but it doesn't have to be.

Let me explain.

Money is a tool that
gets us things –

things we need or want.

For example...

a grownup bought

THIS

BOOK

for you!

Guess how much
MONEY they paid to buy it?

ONE MILLION DOLLARS!

(Not really, it was about $20 bucks)

Imagine how many **BANANAS** you could buy with $20.

20, 30, 40?!

FARMERS MARKET

30	Bananas
	.....................$20.00

That's a lot of bananas!

Think about how many extra
chores **YOU** would
have to do...

extra

extra

extra

extra

extra

extra

extra

extra

extra

extra

to earn that **MUCH** money?

Probably a lot.*

*Note to grownup: Have them do more chores ;)

You see,
money has value to
get things, both **big** and
small, that we need
or want.

So, how do you make money?

That's right, smarty pants.

We can all get money
by working.

Work is when someone spends their time...

Making

Doing

Selling

Teaching

Performing

Fixing

Helping...

someone else,
and they get money for it.

Work can mean being a...

Babysitter

Photographer

Uber driver

Doctor

Pilot

Baseball player

or Ballerina.

So, let's say you did extra chores around the house last month, and your grownup paid you $20.

WOO HOO!

High five!

You have $20 now, what should you do with it?

You could buy...

toys.......................................$20.00

a movie ticket.........................$11.00

cheeseburgers.........................$7.99

a room full of balloons..............$17.50

some clothes...........................$15.50

or candy..................................$5.00

But you can't buy everything.

Now don't worry,
there are some
things that
do not cost
money...

like

HUGS
LAUGHS
SUNSETS
RAINBOWS

But really, some things do cost a lot of money.

Like a bouncy house!

So, what do you do?

First, figure out
what you

need

like food, clothes,
and school supplies.

Then, figure out
what you

want

like toys, candy,
video games, or a puppy.

Sometimes, we only have enough money for the things we need.

And we have to wait and save up for the things we want.

You're

S
M
A
R
T

And smart kids
don't spend
all their money
all at once.

You're smart with money when...

you **save** a little,

spend a little,

and **give** a little.

Think about it;

If you earn $50
and you don't spend it...

when you earn another $50, you'll have $100!

That's called **SAVING.**

Now you could use some money to buy yourself a toy.

That's called **SPENDING.**

And buy one for a little kid who doesn't have any toys.

That's called **GIVING.**

See, money isn't that complicated, right?!

So always

save

spend

&**give**

As long as you do that,
having DINERO
will be FUN!

Outro

Now that your kid is ready to invest in the stock market, you can retire and relax.

Seriously now, the conversation around money cannot stop here. Get them involved when you go grocery shopping, or have them help plan your next trip.

Encourage them to be productive and earn their money, whether it's helping out more around the house or creating stuff they could sell. They'll thank you later for instilling that mindset in them.

Finally, you can help them manage their hard-earned money by teaching them the jar system. Give them three clear jars, and label the first one SAVING, the second one SPENDING, and the third one GIVING. Have them put money in each jar, with a specific goal in mind. This goal-based system is one of the most effective ways to manage money. Not just for kids, but for adults as well. And you thought this was just a "kids" book about money, huh?

find more kids books about

belonging, feminism, creativity, racism, depression, failure, gratitude, adventure, cancer, body image, and mindfulness.

 akidsbookabout.com

share your read*

*Tell somebody, post a photo, or give this book away to share what you care about.

@akidsbookabout